C
COLONY
L
L
A
P
DISORDER
E

Other works by Keith Flynn

Poetry

The Talking Drum (1991)
The Book of Monsters (1994)
The Lost Sea (2000)
The Golden Ratio (2007)

Nonfiction

The Rhythm Method, Razzmatazz and Memory:
How To Make Your Poetry Swing (2007)

Recordings

Swimming Through Lake Eerie (1992)
Pouch (1996)
Nervous Splendor (2003)
LIVE at Diana Wortham Theatre (2011)

C
COLONY
L
L
A
P
DISORDER
E

Keith Flynn

WingsPress

San Antonio, Texas
2013

Colony Collapse Disorder © 2013 by Keith Flynn

First Edition

Printed Edition ISBN: 978-1-60940-294-5
ePub ebook ISBN: 978-1-60940-295-2
Kindle ebook ISBN: 978-1-60940-296-9
Library PDF ebook ISBN: 978-1-60940-297-6

Wings Press
627 E. Guenther
San Antonio, Texas 78210
Phone/fax: (210) 271-7805

On-line catalogue and ordering:
www.wingspress.com
All Wings Press titles are distributed to the trade by
Independent Publishers Group
www.ipgbook.com

Library of Congress Cataloging-in-Publication Data:

Flynn, Keith.
  Colony collapse disorder / Keith Flynn. -- First edition.
     pages cm
  ISBN 978-1-60940-294-5 (pbk. : alk. paper) -- ISBN 978-1-60940-295-2
(epub ebook) (print) -- ISBN 978-1-60940-296-9 (kindle ebook) (print) --
ISBN 978-1-60940-297-6 (library pdf ebook) (print)
  1. Voyages and travels--Poetry. I. Title.
  PS3556.L875C65 2013
  811'.54--dc23

                         2013000740

In memory of

Hayden Carruth

and

David Foster Wallace

CONTENTS

Preface

The title of this collection is taken from the strange oc-currence, discovered in 2006, that began to happen to America's honeybees. Colonies that were once thriving suddenly went still, almost overnight. The worker bees that make hives run simply dis-appeared, their bodies never to be found. Over the next couple of years, nearly one-third of all honeybee colonies collapsed this way, which led to a straightforward name for the phenomenon: colony collapse disorder. These tiny systems looked like the after-math of a World War I battlefield. Everywhere there were shiny, bombed-out, pockmarked ruins. The bees' guts, which should have been white, were stippled brown with infection. Their sting glands had blackened with rare fungal infestations, deformed wing vi-rus, black queen cell virus, Israeli acute paralysis virus, all being delicately handed over by varroa mites which ate their way into the worker. The bees didn't have one disease. They had them all. And the few bees to survive were reeling, and wandering, without purpose, like survivors of a terrifying apocalypse. Great lobes of the hive mind had died, and without any organizing principles, the populations were lost. When you realize that 80% of our food relies on pollination at some point in its life cycle, you can see how this little creature has been referred to as "the landscape architect of the American pastoral." This perfect storm of viruses also ac-counts for the 15 to 20 billion dollars that farmers were losing each season from unpollinated crops.

It occurred to me that this was an ideal metaphor for our current global circumstance. As the great colonial powers slowly topple, they have left in their wake a host of impossible situations. Great Britain alone, as the empire crumbled, was responsible, in whole or in part, for the civil wars in Sri Lanka, Kashmir, Iraq, Sudan, Palestine, Somalia, and Nigeria. What great Mother

Russia has wrought in the eastern bloc countries when she was still a Soviet bear, fighting over the spoils with the other World War II powers, is easy to demonstrate. And we can't leave out Uncle Sam whose covert presence in Chile, Guatemala, El Salvador, Vietnam, Korea, Haiti, Iran, Lebanon, and Afghanistan have worsened the lives of those populations. And as 30 to 40 percent of the advanced world powers move from the Industrial Age into the Information Age, what happens when the remaining two-thirds of the world want the bang for their buck that their colonizers enjoyed for a century? How do we manage the dialogue, or aid the suffering countries, who only now see their way toward a viable market economy in Toffler's *Third Wave*, dictator or democracy, pollution or equality be damned? How does Europe manage the ticking population bomb of Islam? America was once a brown country and will be again in less than two decades. And what of Africa, the long-neglected shame of the world, only now laying off the chains from centuries of oppression, and ripe for the picking as the US, India, China, Russia, Western Europe, and Brazil wade in for their piece of the diamonds, coal, oil, and other mineral resources?

The poems in this book are built in a circular fashion like a Mayan calendar; its architecture and interconnected narrative have a hive mind, with each poem connected to the poem in front and behind it by a theme, an image, or a single word. *Colony Collapse Disorder* is a place-based abecedarium in which each letter of the alphabet is represented by two places, cities, countries, or regions whose name corresponds to the letter and its assigned poem. The poem may be inspired by the place or its traditions, written with geography's characteristics in mind, or it can be aimed at the place, or may take the irony of the place and nestle its rhythm next to the future that is drifting inexorably closer. There are a wide variety of forms and textures, but all 52 poems correspond with the weeks of the year, and interlock the entire collection with historical vignettes. Each attempts to capture a sense of what a worker bee might see through the eyes of a human, how the various places might feel and think through their gauze of feuds or appetites or vanities. Poetry is language with a shape, and a music all its own, my hope is that these shapes bring the reader along, around the world in eighty or so pages, and to feel as if they are completely at home between its covers, bent toward the horizon with a new awareness of the other spirits that are occupying their hive.

C

COLONY

L

L

A

P

DISORDER

E

On the Boardwalk

Sequestered in Atlantic City
where Dinah Washington flirted
with Billy Eckstine at The Blue Orchid
and every lightning-streaked storm
mumbled its pea gravel of rain
and grumbled out to sea.

Where I bought a classical bust
of a woman with a mirror for a face,
never broke down at the blackjack altar,
tabled my expectations, and all were met
as the Ukranian doctor confronted
the Nigerian slugger.

Where the realm of the gull and piper
perfectly intersected with the boardwalk
and its candy factories of nubile
Oriental dolls and steed-mounted
Genghis Khans, in Brooks Brother armaments,
holstered Shamanic come-ons as lions of industry.

Where the petite angel of my dreams
pouted in her sleep on a Puerto Rican flag
while the bitter antibiotic of my seed
glazed her rising breasts, and art deco
trumped the disposable concrete tower,
cranes managed by Mexicans charging by the hour.

Where the dollar is hidden and is King,
seeping through the shell-streaked sediment
minute by minute, where the soul, clenched
in its shell, admires the body's muffled heartbeat,
trailing the dribbled potency of the moment
like cheap perfume, where the Tropics meet

the Hamptons and both succumb, where
the prelapsarian middle class of all rotted
American Dreams comes to be fleeced
and calls it fun, where the spiral helix
of our DNA is mounted and washed gospel
clean, licked by so many tongues.

Rembrandt's Mirror

When the money first comes it seems a waterfall of silk.
The aristocrats want their likeness to display a mauzy gaudiness,
lest they be confused with the riffraff, but reflecting the discipline
and sobriety of a good Protestant employer. Easy to grease
the portal when you're gazing in the mirror and pluck

yourself a doe-eyed, pudding-faced daughter of fortune,
and fill your castle with artistic indisposables, stuffed armadilloes
and historic spears. But when the patron cannot find himself
in your eyes, the vision becomes opaque, the paint layered on,
and the tribal elder becomes the young sophisticate.

Refinement is the catchword of the day, Italian baubles
and Grecian columns, and when a council of your contemporaries
is given the heavenly opportunity to sit in judgement of you,
it becomes a drunken wilding of merry men in the forest clearing,
the fire lighting from below their night watch of long knives.

And when you are stripped of every possession save your mirror,
just big enough for one man to carry, it's like all predictable things.
Cotton-colored moths fly out of the barren closet, youths toss clods
at disreputable fellows whose names are spoken in hushed tones by
their gloating fathers. In the shop windows the splendid visage blurs.

All that is left to paint is tender ugliness; the eloquence of splattered
glass, mercy shavings from the ostentatious tree, balanced above modest
stacks of Christmas gifts, with balled ornaments in the darkened room
clinging to the boughs, whose mirrored surfaces fill with your shadow
and shatter, razored carols waiting for your bare feet to clatter through.

European Political Discourse and the Paranoid Style

What small harm there was
now saturates the greater good.
A vivid first feast of wind,
purity in the form of coercion,
lards the crisp air with recognition,

and those tarred thereafter harden
with resolve. Success has many fathers,
they say, but failure is an orphan.
Their tolerance crusts and sizzles
underneath the lava fall,

congealing into new real estate
as the calamity recedes.
But Berlin still bears the shadow
of the wall, and the tribal
convulsions secrete their hopeful

flares, fomenting inside the wrinkled
features of trusting immigrants, who
brick by brick, build their ghettos
from the remnants of the State's
failed experiments, and ride to work

in the back of the bus, whose
righteous anger explodes a cafe,
or fills the subway with terrible gusts.
Who were proud to be present
when the Great Wall fell, they say,
and then it fell on us.

Gaudí

We cannot tell if we are swimming
among the branches or the roots,
the doorways open into clear blue sky.
The tree outside the window is my teacher,
he said, and Barcelona, she is mine.
Jellyfish float through our bedroom
like lamps carried by parishioners
through catacombs. Catalonian rock faces,
whirlpools and eddies, brazen dragon scales,
clouds on the move; these were the building's

skin-tight costumes. The room's penumbra,
doors opening one into the other, torrents
of tile, and the whale's interior as imagined
by Jonah, shot through with layers of light.
Haloes of wrought-iron palm fronds explode
into space and warn the fence to listen.
The gold and olive ivy climbs translucent
stairs and spires of coral swirl, littered
with saints, all in a jumbled muscular
column toward Heaven. Marble fish

are sliding one against another, sleek silk
tapestries of fin and bone that follow
the sky train to the mountaintop monastery
of Montserrat, whose cliffs were cracked
by the clap of the Crucifixion. Deep thickets
of pleasure, with steel guardians, frolic
around the parlor like nickel-plated cats.

The heart of God is grazed by the fountain's
feathers. Teeth like torches come flying from
underwater and sink into the hillside.

The hinges of the city loosen and shift,
cars disappear into tunnels, like coins in
cake batter, and land in the dancing park.
The windows burst, mouths opening.
Barcelona's frescoes sing and sing, but
the buildings are stillborn, already
weathered by wind and rain, the future
constantly erected in God's honor,
canceling Time's appointment with decay.

Nearing Havana

(being watched by a soldier)

On the plaza the faces of the young girls
like geranium petals on a brackish pond.
The barrier between twilight and nightfall
is filled with the ghosts of the Revolution,
an armada of American cars from the fifties,
like a bounty of white blood cells flooded
into the body as a defense against oblivion.

Unseen stairs and the lethality of armored
illusions cause the myth of the world to swell
as the streets swarm around my heavy shell.
The East Germans say that the Chinese
should understand Berlin; they have the
Great Wall, constructed with copious amounts
of peasant blood over nineteen centuries.

Something within that doesn't trust a fence,
sees a pathway in a pile of bricks,
cannot find the green reed in the white mist.
I have not seen the sun go down from the steps
of the Acropolis, but I have disappeared into
the purple flare of a sunset beneath Clinch Mountain.
The country is a shadow whose words are overcast.

The Cuban horizon is closing fast,
and in a godless country, the citizenry
has learned to row away from the rocks.

Three girls in their funeral dresses
search the city dump for discarded baby chicks
tossed down from the hatchery on the hill.
Sometimes what is lost wants to be found.

The black and white photos show happy rebels
in fatigues kissing the ground. There is no road
built upon the sea, nothing to unknot the shifting
tides of memory, where the litter of promises
makes the mind go wild. In the beginning
was the Revolution, and death followed
behind it like a nursing child.

Speaking In Tongues: The Diaries of St. Pinocchio

I

Coupled with a lacquer of forgiveness,
I keep several versions of the Truth
at the ready. "Don't let them kill us,"
the baby dolls cried; but my hands
were the enemy and would fly into
evil before my mind could catch up.
I could have done it once, but now
I can't go back to being silent, and
I am a child in this new country who
has forgotten my own language and
can speak nothing but yours. Only
hours before Gepetto loosed me from
the log, I told the carpenter not to hit
me too hard. Unsettling as this was,
he forgot and carved an ear onto my head.
I heard Gepetto's poverty and vain
mocking liberties with the Truth, his
golden wig a dead give-away, until he
tripped over me and I banged his shins,
felt the skin of his fingers in my open
mouth, feeling for my tongue. That would
have been enough, but with the bonus of
legs, me and the Devil had to dance.

II

I took my first best chance when the cops
busted Gepetto for shaking me down.
I pedaled home to his studio on a stolen bike,
made my dislike of his paintings fully known
with my own strokes of blown color, my fury
unearthed, then I heard the tedious chirp of
little Jiminy, a tiny black cricket who had
haunted this hut for a century, and admonished
me with vague platitudes about rebellion
and skipping school, but I mashed him
with a mallet and thought nothing of it;
his splatter didn't matter, 'cause I didn't
hang around to visit with the other kids,
or do the things they did. My spirit was
clearly loosed; and I knew what I must do.

III

The nose thing began unexpectedly,
looming off my face in the middle of
a minor misadventure, but soon I
perfected its pitch. Like a fly fisherman,
I could slowly throw it out a safe distance,
even when I was telling the Truth,
to throw my mark off the scent, or
to upset the tension during a plea-filled
soliloquy, I might change the tint
of my skin or grow the nose a bit.

Timing is the essence of Tragedy,
after all, and panic can be your friend.
In the square I danced and fenced and
did my flips. My hands came off with
the gloves, which shook up the poor
peasants who slaughtered chickens
until their arms were sore. Braced
and balder, I stood taller beneath
the thunder crunch of laughter, and
wine always made the whiny curses
of Gepetto fade completely away.

IV

Sure I look pathetic now, no one hoists
you on their shoulders for telling the Truth.
Before I was a boy, my voice was all I had,
and only when settled in wood was I able
to convince Gepetto to free me. Even now
when I leap the brook, it will snatch my
voice and force me to chase it until I stand
beneath the waterfall and it soaks back
into my throat. The old red oak had stolen
my finest notes, the only song I knew,
until I burned him through and through,
muscles of fire, orange and blue,
consumed the tree, freeing my song
to return to me. Once, after my voice
jumped a crow and flew for days with
the bird's black wings, did I think of
giving up and never saying a thing,

just let my actions speak, but clearly
Gepetto enjoyed that crow pie as
much as me and told me how he
longed for my song, though my dance
was fine. The old man delighted
at my sarcastic lines and would always
take care to pay me my share, when
the crowd begged the puppet to sing.

V

Hey, I've been a donkey without shoes,
chipped hooves and sour straw and it's
the reality that gets you every time.
Find a dime on the road and some
toad-faced rabbit talks you out of it,
or better yet, says bury the money and
through some bit of hoodoo honey in
the Land of Miracles you'll be stinking
rich, all your foibles forgotten and gold
in your teeth. Focus for a second on the
scene brewing in the street and fire will
take your feet. Try popping up and down
on them pegs for a second and you'll
start praying for strings and fingers
and forget all about who's really running
the show. We're all a hungry stomach
from the boneyard or the ash box, ain't
no blue fairies floating down all Catholic.
We're just sent here to wait, and God
takes his sweet time, like a snail on

a railing, he's got all day, plays flute
with the fishes, and blows the sky all
out of whack. It's sad really, and I'm
too damn hollow to get all misty on you.

VI

Onstage it's Dream City, and whatever
spell is cast by the deities there, rings in
the dreamer's cuckoo skulls for all eternity.
Poison yourself with a wish and every
swishing tail is yours for the taking.
I'm not making this up, you get in first
person and the crowd's collective yawp
will swallow you like a gum ball. Fall in
line and the royal we can do anything.
I get my suspenders tight, shoe buckles
bright, and we talk down to them poor
fools who paid their fee to see us perform,
hot-wired to the puppet master who speaks
in adoring tones, worn records riding their
familiar groove. First one moves, gets it,
I squeal, and I down the applause like tonic,
the chorus line, the pitter patter of my little
feet, the old man's pride and joy, and I
look in the mirror like everyone else,
100 percent flesh and blood, mimicking
the teacher, but I'm just a boy, I say,
can't you see, a boy, a boy, a boy.

The Exile

This is my last letter. The first one
disappointed in a love triangle has
lost the game. Some things upon
which I've aimed were undoubtedly
innocent; but that is for others to decide.
I've tried to rope the world in countless
ways and have done the best I can,
with tangled prayers and no reprieve.
The danger in the Beast is its seasons.

The morning star enlightened Buddha
and his first words formed a poem
out of the desperate ardors,
adders made of words, blind as a boxer,
striking out at every sound.
How do we discriminate?
The map is linear, but poetry is
circular and continuous,
untangling as it tells.

Alabama Chrome

There is no crime of which
I cannot conceive myself guilty.
                    —Goethe

Hard to explain away
Holy Ghost power ripping at a tongue,
or a pig boiling in a vat of shine,
duct tape holding together
a Malibu, shading a dog asleep
beside a possum skull chewed down
to the bone and the sheen
on that tape is Alabama Chrome.

Still waters house cottonmouth nests
and test the depths of an Easter
baptism by a West Virginia
coal mine apostle handing out
Holy Roller popsicles and New
Testaments, two for a dollar.
His shoes have holes in the soles
and carry a satchel with crosses
made out of Alabama Chrome.

Pompadours signify a trickster
made slicker with a combful
of axle grease, trees stripped
beneath a dozer like matchsticks
rolled in the teeth of fourteen
illegal Mexicans handing tobacco
in a ramshackle locust post lean-to,

and the odor of fajitas that smells
like home, six inch shoulder gash
held together with Alabama Chrome.

Tattoos with more cover-ups
than a DC barrister, maimed
fingers and feet and acetylene
torches forming Jesus sculptures
for sale at the healing, six miles
from the border, out of the trunk
of a Buick Regal, whose busted
quarter panel testifies to the enduring
strength of a live oak, growing alongside
the sacred swamp, whose gentle nature
belies the road sign on its trunk, mile
marker formed by strips of Alabama Chrome.

Handsome warlocks, strapped to strip
malls, and mauled by the perfection
of the window shows, grow stories
packed with prison grits and sugar tits
and drop poison pellets from their
raven beaks onto the lips of sun-streaked
Meth-pocked blondes in the windy
parking lots of ritualistic pawn shops
and close-cropped itchy trigger teeth
gritted in the Marine recruiting station,
whose volunteers choose grief over
nothing, and shaving lotion in their
sweaty palms help jack the microphones
on the parade podium, faulty wiring saved
once again by a slab of Alabama Chrome.

First there's a funeral, then a trial,
judges killing time with stretchy statutes,
whose busted claws grow back in
a generation like crawdads, whose only
sin is proximity to poverty, and fractured
fairy tales with family trees raised
on probation, and sentenced to speaking
in tongues, are gigged on Confederate
cinderblocks, cut and shot with
Pentecostal backslides, artistic outlaw
fanatics, whose sexual gymnastics atop
cigarette machines crack the secular
windows of the gray institutions, and
no reflection is shown, with holes sealed
up and renovated with Alabama Chrome.

The Future of an Illusion

In El Paso, Texas, mid-August, 1982,
and it is so hot the trees are chasing
the dogs around, muggy as donkey guts.
This must be where the Devil goes
on vacation, I think, marooned in a brown
Chevy van, parked sideways in an alleyway,
with one eye peeled for the cops,
having a conversation with a prostitute
who is anchoring the bus stop bench. Forty,
with Gladys Knight lips, and fading already,
her last words as she started to pass out,
the proclamation that tonight she would
smoke herself straight into Hell,
downhill all the way. She rolled over
on her sled, as her feet fell asleep first,
and her cigarette dimmed, its slim
crack-laced surface tipped by
a glowing cinder on the end.

I was once shocked by an unconscious act,
of a dying man in near coma, awakened
by fear of a lit cigarette dropping onto his
pillow as he dropped asleep still puffing,
both smoke and cigarette invisible,
but the mouth still sucking. Death is the same,
coming or going. It leaves a hole, doesn't say
please, walks with a swagger and takes its toll,
blows a smoke ring into the fan and watches it roll.
When the pieces fly apart, Death smiles,
feeling the rhythm skip, out of nowhere,

a cloud that's forgotten where it was supposed
to blow, and breaks into shards
that Death swallows whole.

If the spiritual master is a sky
that remembers itself, like Vermeer in Delft,
reducing the world to a pearl earring, then that
is why star after star opens its cylinder
eyes and fires back at us with varied success.
If God lived on Earth, people would break
His windows, egg His barely moving electric car,
step on His robe, and call Him a fag at the mall.
How tall is your defense? Even in the Bible
it's six to five against making it to sunup.
All of the eternal elements must balance.
Yet we forget, and are overwhelmed with
nostalgic fragrances, the furniture of eternity,
a house musty with anger, whose master
moves like mist among the eaves.

The Agnostic

Nature selects for survival, Man, for appearance.
Our behavior evolves according to our needs.
Science, at war with Religion, reveals our origin.

That man is a beast, at least that much is certain;
the battlefields of Nature have never given him ease.
Dung beetles working the carrion, maggots sprung

from their blue black ooze, brutish reproduction
and the survival of louts, intent on spreading their
own versions of honor, duty-bound to lance

the boil of imagination. The loss of faith is a slow
process, like the raising of continents from the eternal
rush of water, and the deposits engendered there,

layer upon layer, trembling with extinction.
What was once a free-swimming creature
finds itself glued by the head to a rock.

Assuming the Conception

My body turned 45 and the wheels
fell off—borderline diabetic, astigmatic,
knee reconstructed, nine concussions,
right foot broken three times,
right fist is a three-time loser
of boxing fractures, collarbone
splintered, groin torn, eczema,
myopia, dystopia, prostate the size
of an Idaho potato.

Flashes under my skin, twinges of,
not pain exactly, but radishes of electricity,
like dandelion nodules of broken fireworks
crackling miles distant on a drive-in screen
right angle to the horizon. I'm falling away
and pitchers of light release their rivulets
into my bloodstream. What pours down
are the sparkling nerves whose roots
and antics attack the symmetry of the
suffering machines' decorous decline.

This design, with carnal exactitude,
like Vesalius' wailing skeleton,
propped on its spade handle
like a crutch, having dug itself up
into this one patch of real estate,
and reminded of this wounded world,
how eternity, in love with all the forms,
throws back its head and cries out.

Lolling about in this Hell,
old bird, your beak numbly clacking,
clenched around a twig whittled
to the size of a cigarette, you will not
succumb to the institution's whitewashed
viral simplicity, its bardic death-head
preoccupied with oxygen counts and
vegetable mush, three a.m. wakeup calls
for morphine's singular dream-like cocoon,

the unrushed guilt, deliberate, final,
and solid as a granite monument,
a sharp-peaked Rocky Mountain looming
silently over the steady drip of the proceedings,
(and all the animal shadows gliding benignly
with great force in the river of darkness below).
O the terrible depth of our disbelief, floating
in the bells of our bodies.

The university of adversity, my father says,
allows us to pile up our compulsions,
and I know we are pegged
end to end, and we are reborn,
our damaged plans trickling
into our aging capillaries.
Emphysema, congestion, shingles,
cirrhosis, ulcers distending the baggage
and balloons of our tubing and viscera.

Dangling there in the bells of our bodies,
lolling in this hellish instant,
what infinite silence envelops us
as the soul sings, finding its voice
in the invisible springs between tones,

the mortar of stillness stiffening,
and my father, a quavering note
who has not risen, lives still.

The Blues

Last night I dreamed of my wife,
two years gone, the traces of feeling
in men, like marble in meat,
the hypnotic interiors that highlight
the soul's confusion, like a moth trapped
in a glass or under a hat on the floor.
Nothing rises, not History which requires two,
or marriage with its schizophrenic feeling,
half longing, half belonging, like living
in a homeland constantly occupied by
a different neighboring country.

                                        Her curls
wind-whipped in a field, the old comfort
of our lust rolling through the weeds
in a Welsh meadow of bluebells, and the
cratered places where our bodies had been,
the weight of absence, or the inertia of images,
the half-traced alcove of a piazza's blueprint,
the eclipse of the moon, the plaster casts
of bodies faced with death, contorted together
in Pompeii beneath an age of ash, a single
feather on a beam of wind from atop Chichen
Itxa fastened alone on a journey to the Mexican
jungle.

        I can feel my eye breaking on the coastal
plain, a piece of shoestring tied to a wire,
the silent mouth screaming in an o-ring of
pleasure or fear, all the questions, curdled milk

streaming from a cracked carton into the waves.
I have wondered, if by these details one could
inhabit or comprehend another, by what method
do we understand the spires of an incomplete
building stabbing out at Time whose face
is hidden?

      Camped on a cliff, can we become
complete as one gull battles a crater of saltwater
with its crushed wing, while the flowers ferment
under concrete pressure, and the smell of a muse
that cannot be viewed, flays with a strange violence
in my brain? The fossils rise, their pearly skulls
drained of local color. There is no coupling
of natures, no merger of worlds.

         The dead name us,
taking the first fork they find and bending it to suit
their own peculiar path. Ever speak of this and their
voices run wild. Just ask anybody, wandering
half-lit by the moon on a country road at night,
where the shadows announce themselves and
disappear, their presence overblown in a land
scape of broken ruses, and the ending is the blues.

Easter in Palestine

On the face of it, the landscape bore
an astounding nostalgia for lies.
The tapestries cried; the gates of Paradise
opened and shut like the jaws of a shark
in the frenzy of chum.

Smoke slumbered over the dumb meters
flickering benignly, their red numbers
exponentially growing, and thus glowing
with greater insignificance as they blossomed.
The bottom cratered accordingly.

Traffic islands drifted in disbelief
among the gray hazards.
Blizzards of bright birds, like opium bubbles,
were gossiped about, but their swallows
capsized, the quills of their wings

bristled and hissed like bicycle spokes.
Navigating the choked imagination,
the jewelry of the Bible tinkled
and dispersed, hard blades of grass
pierced the floor; and the sand was coming.

It sounded like rain in the buckets
and the confused chimes snuck
their songs by clothesline along
the drowning boards, so sweet and calm.
The gourds broke open like psalms.

Election Day at the Grand Canyon

Though something is understood
by the electorate, speaking the language
of the dispossessed, passing its charge
like lightning that assaults the pasture tree
and electrocutes the horses in its shade.
A pinpoint of stillness, restful alertness, cursory
recognition as the epoch shifts, though the canyon
and its rafters both collide with the river
and the red walls are unmoved. "Love bade me
welcome yet my soul drew back," wrote Herbert,
with typical twitchy syntax. What changes
is the will to change, the estrangement of prior faith,
every man a moon with a dark side that doesn't show
through, a black hidden fuse waiting to be lit,
revealed in fits and false starts.

What person would want to be President,
to stand with age shock in the gateway of Death,
becoming the business of the busybody
in a nation of finks, as ogled as the Mona Lisa,
with her inscrutable smile and Madonna iconography,
priceless and precisely mysterious? In America
we steer with frontier irreverence and mistake it
for affection, our austere offices, cornered and waiting,
caves that mortgage, with shrinking dividends,
the primitive imagination. In these broken places,
weighted by the freight of commerce,
the stalled mules nick one another from boredom.
Goaded with switches and curses,
they glide into the canyon with borrowed buoyancy,
shirking against the gravity of their loads.

A Navel in the Middle of the World

I

The sea a mood indigo,
with frothy lips, and Miami
receding on the event horizon,
a conga line of steel skeletons
waiting for their skin,
where one cormorant,
the size of Goliath,
nested & hunted from atop
the construction crane,
like a live gargoyle,
making at night
his fantastic silhouette,
Luftwaffe wingspan
inspiring men to put
his likeness in their poems
and on their money.
South, the Cayman Islands,
in concert with the Gulf's
warm undercurrent, lubricate
Labadee, fat and warm.

II

Bon appetit, like a navel
in the middle of the world,
but the quasi slow motion
gut punch of an earthquake
has embedded lifting landscapes
and levitating statues, pigeons
frozen above confused fountains,
and buildings falling from their
place in the air, like a woman
slowly dropping her slip from
one shoulder as she sidles away.
All this in the collective
unconscious of the suddenly
homeless residents who have
no plan for the future and all
conversations contain elements
of the past tense and God,
they say, has completely
flattened into rubble what
once was Labadee.

The Director

The movie is an instrument of pleasure. . . .
—Alberto Lattuada

Looking out the villa window,
centered above his desk,
the sea is a kind of eternity;
its endless anonymity is a relief
and a horror. He was a Sunday child,
born on the national Independence Day,
(every nation has one) and the son
of a vicar and a vixen,
scandal in his DNA.

One escapes dissolution through
lies and deception, the first
and most creative instinct
that a child develops.
Perjury prevents injury,
or deflects it, surviving the slanted
homestead's Hall of Gravity.

Sympathetic and clear-sighted
executors of the regime
balance on stilts. Senators, parading
as parents, erect the scaffolding of the Law
around the boy's architecture.
The first one tears down the steel,
joint by joint, to plan his departure

HOLLYWOOD • CALIFORNIA

and lay tracks for his train,
making of his work a chaos
that he might nestle in.
Even the demons should be harnessed
to the wagon, said Bergman,
and pedagogic eruptions keep
the chatter down. The births
of his children, the court dates,

the wives, the larger checks one was
required to sign, filter in and out
independent of the calendar or almanac.
What one makes or avoids makes
escape a strategy, lethargy the only
cancer whose trap might hold.
How does one hunt for home?
We allow ourselves everything and then

nothing will suffice, curing ourselves
of the ability to distinguish.
The movie screen unfurls kiss after kiss,
miles of film spinning on harnessed reels;
the white hats win, the black ones
barter with annihilation,
and by not sleeping, learn
to practice dying every day.

In the evening, sitting on the porch,
the lilac hedge trumpets open unnoticed.
The sunsets file away pixel by pixel.
The nails loosen in the eaves, serenaded
by duende and the wind's somber doves.
One sits down at the desk.
The desk must be tidy.
The holes are everywhere.

Lincoln's Life Mask

Who would guess, 150 years hence,
that visitors would line up to look you
in the eye? Staring face to face with
Lincoln, that square Midwestern
Clint Eastwood chin, every profile
from the right, excepting two, his first
campaign poster, and the cartoon of his
assassination, shanghaied from behind
by Booth.
      Nearby is the smallest book
in the world, containing the poems of
Edgar Guest, a book in a bottle that would
fit in Lincoln's mole, and the entire engraved
plate collection of Audubon, a miracle itself,
reminding one that Lincoln once shot a wild
turkey through a crack in the cabin wall.
"Who knows what lie they will buy?" Booth
thundered. One man's president is another
man's emperor.
      Audubon never painted
a penguin, and Lincoln and Darwin were born
on the same day, on opposite sides of a dream.
Outside is a totem pole made of light, beaming
its one pure eye into space. With a wink, Lincoln
charmed Grant into silence, and Darwin stood,
staring God down, both refusing to blink.

The Birth Mark

Sex is exposure
and fur is not.
The slipper has
no place in the
slaughterhouse.
The same water
that cleanses, kills,
and the will
that erases the
coward, will make
him take a bullet
for his friend.
Justify the world
and be confounded.
That is the first law.

Gray Power

Tangled, whistling past my wishes,
I don't look back with irony
at my devolution, or with the
Sisyphean tyranny of a dinner
theater poetry reading, navel-gaze
with jaunty pessimism about
my middle-aged dysfunction.

Just as no one becomes depraved
all at once, the accumulation
of sounds make the poem,
claws scraping, windows breaking,
the lowing cow or guttural bassoon.
Balloons bog past filled with gas,
and the heat remembers long pleats

of bird wings, leaf shimmers,
loose-headed hammers singing
from the hillside. I cycle inside
my own zone of silence, my own
bell tong frozen in its parabola,
drooping upside down in a cup
emptied of sound, with gray tones

attacking my camouflaged position.
So much happens in an instant,
the red daze in the eye of the raven
as it falls on the wick of a bug.
Blue mold gathering in the wall
waits for rain. The latitudes and
longitudes of pain spread along

the nerve endings of every living thing.
The moon waxes and wanes; waves faint
against the rocks. A camel cocks his head
and hears the wind crawl across the sand,
prelude to a storm. Warm water begins
to change in the kettle. The lost energy
of steam is leaving a million chimneys;

and I am chosen by some gray power
to listen and explain, though it is May
and the mind is marooned, sinuses pouring,
full with the excretions of blossoms,
blessed pollen borne aloft on the legs
of bees. How beautiful I think,
between sneezes, this reasoning,

these seasons, that purple thistle thorn
poised one inch from the beating heart
of a hummingbird in its frantic hover,
its spectral beak glazed with honeydew,
the embodiment of ambition and reflection
and the butterfly's burden, to unfold
its flickering tableau for this small poet,

unleashing typhoons on the other side
of silence, risking discovery by virtue
of its flight, erased by the cascade of night,
dropping its copper twilight curtain
in a billion rooms whose souls flicker
for an instant with defeat in the growing
dark, and then agree to go on.

The Seven Islands of Izu

Wind through wood
makes a sound,
whistles through rock,
or squeals on the leaf edge.

The hardest wind
wants something
to push down,
or mass against,

and in every chest
cavity, the answering
heart beats out its life,
buried in bone.

*

The oars row
and the water opens,
tense and flexible.
The boat is held

between the water's
fingers and squeezed
toward land.
Two sticks, in both fists,

make the quivering
limbs fill with
blood and flow
through the air.

Above the floor,
the drums never
seem to tire
of the blows.

The good drum,
like water,
never takes
a breath.

                *

Death is gripped
in the tentacles
of water and
does not care.

In His world
there is no
room for air.
The purity of

the reed and
its song is
disrupted by
a single hair.

                *

There on his neck
the man feels
a watery breath
and lunges forward,

swinging his two
fists filled with air.
The singer is
released by a push

of wind. The dancer
is delivered by
the sticks, attacking
the drumskin for

its memory of bone.
When the drum
is broken, the
singer is alone

and the band
gathers on each
side. Death is
propelled by

the same force
as life. As the
Light presses down,
Darkness pushes back.

Between them
the drum
keeps time.

The Force of Compassion

Sit with things and listen long
and the singing will begin.
Turn your free fall into
a voluntary act. The song
shattered, every being
takes its piece of the harmony.
The well of the past is bottomless
and in the walls the song climbs
out of the nets and jewels of time,
the infinite unraveling mingled
with bitter intervals of radiance,
well water, lotus heart, rising crane.

Appalachia

Daniel Boone, coming through slaughter,
Is inexplicably drawn to another standard.
Fourteen painted figures, with eerie deserted
Cries, form into trees, while brazen spinning
Silhouettes, grazing on the fringe, find
The frontiersman on all fours between two
Rhododendrons, dreaming a railroad into
Being, as gladioli, measured by bees, shiver
Like marmalade in the bestial window.

Carbon pirouettes surround six fly fishermen
Flinging spiderwebs into red water as
Mad shattered cows in fishnet stockings
Swat metallic mosquitoes on the bank.
A true native of this prickly country,
With roots up to my neck, pulling
At these denizens' bitter natures,
Whose final versions of themselves
Contain one skin too few, I accept

The responsibility of vengeance without
A second thought, my sun-stirred
Southern cross hogging its family slice,
Jinx talk making its overture to Orpheus
In the underworld as he plucks the wings
Off another hummingbird to add to his harp's
Veneer and sneers at Daniel Boone
Shooting turtles like skeet on the other
Side of the ever-rising lake of fire.

The Brides of Christ

are not like you and me. Their old habits
are seldom broken. Their self-flagellation
lasts for days. They do not labor under
the curse of death and their bodies,
weighted with grace, do not decompose.

Bernadette bravely chose to address
the Virgin Mary at the cave in Lourdes.
The Sisters of Nevers supported her,
bedridden as she was with a tubercular kneecap.
When the holy water spurted out

like a golden ribbon, the countryside
was bathed in light; scales fell from eyes,
limbs straightened, the ice of chastity
froze the thorns on the trees;
bullets rotted in their barrels.

As for blood, there is always blood,
pouring from the palms or the feet
or for the Sister Adorers of Saint Hyacinth,
their entire robes were soaked
in red remembrance of the final trials

of God on Earth, the Holy Son,
in slow ascent, smelling of lilacs and
ripped to pieces by Roman soldiers,
completely unaware of their place
in history. How lonely to be married

only to Jesus and every day spent
in penance, re-enacting His last
horrible hours as He, step by step,
rose from His labyrinth toward
that body double in the final scene.

Or like Catherine of Sienna, disguised
as Yogi Berra, catching the fast balls
leveled from the untroubled guillotine
and hearing her name uttered by those
fading lips, lifted the lone heads

to her own and kissed them.
Only one soul in these old Heavens
that knows my name, she would say.
If, by praying, we are actually compelled
to listen to a voice not our own, or

merely by listening more intently we
are saved and pray in response, giving
each particle its proper name, then
lifting one's self in prayer might actually
keep the nuns from flying away.

Like Sister Agreda who thwarted
the Inquisition when Conquistadors
confirmed her blue satellite had been
transmitting the salvation story to tribes
in their native tongue half a world

away, her white bat-winged hood
pedaling her doughy visage through
the gray clouds of Northern Mexico.
There is no mediocre life that ends
in exile or is seduced by Baron Von Trapp

and his singing brood of magpies,
hopscotching from hilltop to hilltop, one step
ahead of the Nazis, who, looking for a
crook in every nanny, searched for Jews
in every nook and cranny, aided

by a Pope who looked the other way.
Still the brides of Christ stared down
Vichy and the war, bundled the orphans
and nursed the poor, and now stand
in medieval garb atop the last castle

walls of a machine built to supplant
man's base nature and lift him,
unyielding, into the pastures of forgiveness.
Across the landscape, the nuns come flying
in formation against a wintry sky while

the snow, in lacy breaths, spirals and misfires,
careens in layers brought low by wind,
in patterns that legitimize the proponent's
concerns, that the jigsaw puzzles of God
form a tapestry, a soot-free path into

His thoughts, that the travails and misery
of this world will be traded for the perfection
of another in ratios too abundant
for the human mind to surmise. And so
the convent stands, straddling the past

and future, a forbidding bridge by which
one might fly in surreptitious tones
of snowy surrender, a chaste flake
chastised by mortals, half-melted
already in Heaven's eye.

Henry VIII

She is a singular creature,
Mary, as guileless as Anne
is treacherous, notable
for her integrity as Anne
is for her steel ambition
(and Catherine, which one?).
My romantic notions
are killing this country.
But if God is King
on Earth, to whom do
I answer, Rome or
myself, the people
or me, their conscience?
Who can understand a King?
Other Kings? Who or whom
must I outwit, outlast, outcast,
create, cajole, annihilate?
Whole families and their countries
come at me in waves.
God is silent; perhaps he has
forgotten me, as I have
now obliterated Him.
Heads in baskets are headed
to the smokehouse, if God
is fire, then I will give
Him plenty to burn.

The Perfect Game

Our judgement
is marred by events
less onerous or pernicious
than the legally blind man
bowling a perfect game,
saying how it was like
looking down the barrel
of a flashlight and
just aiming with
repeated steps
at the center of that
circle and if there was
need of a spare then one just
rubbed out the light that was left,
but on that fated day there was no need
to steady the ball or let it drop off the ledge
of his hand into the small shining saucer of water
in the distance, the dance was the thing, the same
measured pocket of hips in sympathetic sway with
the lane, a tango of invisible efficiency and each time
he dipped his partner's head toward the floor all the
pins in the world rattled and fell with a mighty roar
until at last the music fell silent and all the lights were
out and the ball did not magically rise to his fingers
or gravity sprout a dancer to duel in the dark groove
where a cane will take over and nothing disturb
the count of steps to the door or the stubbed-toe
curb, the clock position of food on his plate
or folded corners of money, nothing to take
the place of the line dance and the roll
of the ball, the splatter of perceptions
and the air filled with palpable awe

Rendition and the White Dwarf:
A Handbook for Perpetual War

The official greeter trampled at Walmart,
two shot dead at Toys-R-Us, Black Friday's
retail death toll pales in comparison
to the world's largest city attacked
by Muslim murderers at ten separate
locations simultaneously, pirating ashore
on plundered boats from Pakistan,
leaving blood splatters upon the Taj Mahal.

In a grainy photo, a male figure
in a black hood, with arms outstretched
in surrender or forgiveness,
is perched precariously upon
a milk carton or stump.
Ropes or cables are attached to his
wrists or fingers. It is Macon, Georgia, 1905.

Dwindling in twilight, the blue dress melted,
pouring off her back, and hung there above
the ground without ever wrinkling or landing,
but twinkling like a faded Xmas angel
on the top of a tattered, tinsel-strewn tree,
the seedy evidence a jewel in bas relief,
shining like a baby sun.

Scandal is the music of our age,
its cunning reflexivity and natural
proximity to power and celebrity ensuring
the knee jerk denouement will never come.

That punishment is an inexact science
of knotted evasions and appeals, elevating
the accused mongrel as it prevaricates
and feints, not wrong or right, but worthy
of sympathy or condemnation, criticism
laced with overwrought understanding
of the circumstances and tossed about
like a beach ball by tanned pundits.

A man makes his history by the pieces
he is given, and has no choice, driven by
the felicities of language and the worth
of his station, which he cannot worry
into changing. Subversion becomes
the currency of his tongue. Every fact
is a fiction fleshed with storytellers,
reporters flushed with the excitement
of first commitment, turning like a rotisserie
chicken on their sterile spit, reporting all sides
of the crime until the skin of integrity splits
and the born-on date fades into the mist.

Who could bear up, after all, under the weight
of so much reality? The War on Culture becomes
The War on Drugs becomes The War on Terror,
while the bottom billion are frozen into statues
turned to salt from malnutrition and news fatigue,
shadows burned into the Pulitzer prize-winning
film treatment of the latest atrocity. Absolved,
embedded and beheaded, early morning soldiers
of the coming Apocalypse are herded into
cul-de-sacs of empty promises, and their faith,
lit by gunpowder and Caribou Barbie, overflows.

Nanking, 1937

After they dug the hole,
we lay down one upon the other,
our feet and hands tied
loosely together, the better
to keep us corralled, and we
thought it might be like sleep.
They would just cover us up
and it would be over, but after
a few shovelfuls were tossed in
our mouths and faces, they began
to laugh and pour gasoline in our pit,
and when they lit it, the pain,
like falling through space, and the air
was made of tumbling knives
and broken glass. The burned ones,
by their weight, held the bodies
fast below, half-charred and covered
in melted skin, and many took all
the next day to die. Enough dirt was
tossed to douse the flames on top, and
the bored soldiers were ordered off.
There was a curved rock at the bottom
that I curled against, and on the third day,
I used what was left of my hands to dig
through the stench and wails and jelly
to the surface, and walked
thirty-five miles to tell you this tale.

The Silver Surfer

for Stan Lee

A froth of moon reveals
the hissing river,
                    momentarily
pausing
            for the silver owl
to drop
            on a rabbit and
orchestrate its death curdle.

The roof,
            bathed in a creamy glow,
seems covered in snow,
                        but it is
late August and the white trees
in the waning moonlight
                        are resolute
against the black curtain.
                        The sky
is burning,
            released from its burden,
to buoy
            on its fingertips,
the mythology of a perfect night.

The suicides,
            convinced it is so,
open their veins, step off
                        the building,

or drink down
                    a Milky Way of valium,
each star
            they swallow
                            flooding
their skull with light.
                        I save what I can,
riding the crest of ever-
                        collapsing darkness,
trying to catch
                the unbroken bodies
                in my arms.

The Night Train to Omega

We're worn out. Nobody reads poetry
anymore, but everyone writes it.
Seven students, haunted by parables
and anthems, holistically convene
in the woods to find any words
that are still alive. Don't need

to believe that the Bible is God's
living word to believe that the living
word is God. James Brown would concur.
We are standing by the tracks, juking
with the porters in South Carolina,
waiting for the Night Train.

In Sri Lanka you can train an elephant
to carry your surfboard. The silver birch
trees in Poland look like aluminum baseball
bats, water beads on them. The Lake of Heaven
resembles the iris of God, the same blue paint
a shaman uses to streak his nose in the Bering Strait.

On the Night Train from New Orleans,
with Teddy Pendergrass yowling like
an alley cat in the seat beside me, his
disembodied voice on the DVD delighting
the Panamanian grandpa who bounces
the image on his lap like a baby.

The average heart beats 4300 times in an hour,
and lightning strikes the Earth 25 million times a year.
Imagine you have been struck by lightning, I tell
my students, and your dearest memories
are gone, replaced by a growing super power.
12 people in Russia killed by lightning just this week.

From Belleville to DC on the Night Train,
a chocolate mother nursing her black baby
with Kool-Aid from an aluminum bottle.
Little angel's wings dropped off in Richmond,
and the singing infant's full throat flung open.
Every noise is not joyful, my friends.

Every two seconds, somewhere in the world,
a Tupperware demonstration begins.
Every year 2000 more McDonalds open
their doors and Ronald opens his arms
in a Jesus Christ pose, with the clothes
and hairstyle he stole from Bozo.

Every artist is subject to a master's phase,
I exclaim, but stand in praise of the accident,
stand in praise of the mixed couple hunching
in the kitchen car restroom, paddling their
bloom-filled boats upon the track that pulls
our wracked skins northward on the Night Train.

In Muynak, Uzbekistan abandoned ships sit
hull-deep in sand at the edge of what was
once the Ural Sea. A copper-colored orangutan
in Kalimantan, Borneo, sits calmly in a blue rowboat
eating a banana, waiting for his trainer to return.

There are no famous writers, I tell the acolytes,
only famous re-writers eliminating waste.
Listen, I repeat, listen with your whole being.
On the Night Train from Greenville to New
York City, I fell asleep in Baltimore and awoke
in Rheinbeck alongside the Hudson, a bald eagle
keeping vigil on a rotted marsh log.

The Blue Teen on Train 52

Cut the umbilical cord with her teeth
and wrapped it in tissue paper,
slowly walked out of the stall
and laid it gently atop the day's trash,
tried to make it as much of a ritual
as she could, with her body hypersensitive
to every brush of air. The hawk's one wing
steering down was loud as a car alarm,
the brakes of the tires shifting and squealing
around her as she crossed the street;
the subway train and its steel was
excruciating, so much sound and panic
so that when the cabin emptied and the
wheels made their monotonous clack,
the feeling was of regularity and routine,
like living inside the womb of a giant clock
and listening to the tonic of its tick made
the body woozy and full, buoyed and blocked
atop the pillowy tock, rocked in the arms
of time and taken from stop to stop.
As the blood pushed out and pooled
there was no one or nothing to slow
the body's pulsing, no elbows or shoving,
no buzzing or blurting, nothing to alert
the cameras or shirts, swishing on
the platforms above comfortable shoes
and the day's bad news about the stretcher's
failed rescue of the blue teen on train 52.

The Resurrection of Haute Couture

Chanel

Glamour puss loved her fat cats.
Ugliest parts of the body, knees.

Lagerfeld

Fashionistas, as long as Chanel exists.
American, German, English, all need Paris.

Christian Lacroix

Even in Uzbekistan, Couture is Civilization.

Christian Dior

Soft shoulders, full busts, fine waists
like vines, wide skirts like petals.

One pencil lowers forty million hems.

Poiret

No gilded cages, wife without corset,
Pope Pius punted pink slave pantaloons.

If someone is simply a couturier,
then all you do is sew
slinky sheaths opting for nipple exposure,
with champagne flowing in your veins.

In painting, Picasso. In fashion, Poiret.

The dress just says it all.

Givenchy

Oui, Audrey petite, 31-22-31
Her mannequin, means for me, perfection.

Vionnet

Silk-crepe, cut to the bias,
(powdered pubic hair preserving smooth lines),
Euclidean purist, sewing the body electric.

Valentino Red

How does one commandeer a color?

Balenciaga

Parisian fabric roses, breathing very hard.

Pierre Cardin

Master of Licensing, meet George Jetson!

Michael Kors

Caviar Kaspia wedded to Burger King,
perfect melds of intelligence and artifice.

Dignity's bottom gauntlet, pop-cult tsunamis.
Good-bye Celine, Hello Michelle Obama...

Yves Saint Laurent

Rocket's red glare, ready to wear,
a tempest in a B-cup.

Le Bal Crillon

Sheltered debutantes trade rattles for saddles.
Famous fine dresses for clothes horses,

good luck hair in the hemline.
Suicidal princesses missing Best-Dressed Poll.

Diana Vreeland

Mundane mannequins seeking elegance, not relevance.

My husband's bankruptcy, ten dresses only...

Brigitte Bardot

Fake chiffon panties for stylish grannies.

Empress Eugenie

Every woman wants to be Beauty.

Of Beasts, the wildest is woman.

Jackie O

One dress, no other woman existed.

Galliano

At this altitude, we drive differently.

Nan Kempner

Bury me in a dress box.

Extraordinary Popular Delusions
and the Madness of Crowds

for Charles MacKay, 1841

After the men shot the pillows
full of smoldering holes
they started on the windows
glass showered on the food and drink
but the dancing and shooting continued
pistols pointed at the ceiling
the chandeliers came down
the dogs ran
the revelers opened fire on the clouds
'til rain came in sheets
the empty rifles had umbrellas
in the barrels
the men swirled laughing
the war is over they shouted
as they danced the houses into rubble
and killed the cows to feed the party
the war is over they cried
when their legs gave out
they used the rifles for crutches
and continued to shout
blood for blood they screamed
the code of the clan
for fifteen centuries
they squeezed and squeezed
the triggers when their bullets ran out
though there was nothing left to kill
if the lion does not tell the story
then the hunters certainly will

Using the Enemy's Arrows

I like to take a line for a walk,
try it for truth among the oaks.
The depths emerge from a glut of dreaming
and the sorting of seeds, the minutes of days.
If told, its scale focuses through guise
and does not do, but collapses and cannot say.
Its guile preys on weeds of weak thread
and clean knees, its glorious, worthless
stages forced on the least-willing participants,
with words of their own they dare not repeat.
It is the story that comes and lathes
its immense reassurance with lost
flushes of pulses and repeated pleasure holds.
Myth is the story of a particular tree
whose roots constitute a great drinking,
and whose trespass is parallel to music.
Those rings, gathered in bridges, let fly
the human course over rivers and space.
Those rings give rhythm and travel light, hide
and collect the enemy's fiery arrows at night.
Why make of an active world this boast,
this wobbly unit of lovely horror, a germ
that sees in every living thing a host?

Facebook

Perhaps I could be the water, she says—almost visible, but ever present.
I am wind, I suppose, apt to knock things over, and always moving—
We feel like two harbors, fed by the same water, in sight of one another,
holding a similar shore...I think I want to mingle my rivers with yours

and then you become a toreador, dodging the white bull of my constant
whimsy— We are just flimsy mutations in love with velocity, and
as the planet wobbles round, our evolution leaps forward and we are
threaded into the millenia like bird songs, a jungle's connective tissue

like the new species found in the last failing year, glass frogs in Ecuador
whose beating hearts throb like tiny artichokes in the beakers of their
transparent bodies, or bluetooth tarantulas in French Guiana with a taste
for birds, five foot penguin fossils discovered in Peru, and an arachnid

in Madagascar whose spun silk is tough as Teflon and lives in Darwin's
dreams of copper bark and tube-nosed fruit bats with Yoda faces whose
undigested seeds get ladled with poop through nocturnal crop sprays;
again diplomatically handling a clearly personal problem with aplomb.

Perhaps I could be the high altitude tree ant, she says, sauntering about
miles above your giant woolly rodent, or a cobalt-colored toad the size
of a pea, with torrid little wings that purred like turbines as I wound
around the breeze of your argument— That'll be the day, I sneeze, when

suddenly she is offline and a bitter taste like turpentine fills the chat space
where she gets the final word on my wall. Two photos containing corrupt
data flow past like a pale virus. Failing to communicate is part and parcel
of the human condition, says a Google advertisement attached to the tail

of a Firefox as spools of invitations from all over the nation regurgitate on
the right column of my home page like ticker tape. She wheezes back to
chat and reminds me that we have not friended though we are clearly
connected, and my sense of humor is expanding, despite my variable

entitled identities vying for space inside her growing sense of privacy,
our shared intimacy a keystroke or two away. There is intellectual back
pedaling and an aborted social performance is yanked from the stage. No
mere peddler, she is appalled, and pulls her punctured persona off in rage.

Without our bodies we cannot love, or kill the messenger or edit the thread.
This platform is just like the Pony Express, with a billion ponies all steaming
at the same time into a town riddled with mirrors, though they are funhouse
glasses at best, constantly morphing like a many-headed Hydra, a barrage

of bait with no waiting, playing with a cosmos of information, embedded
in the parts of our character that cannot change, and our vigilant eyes are
splintered with murmuring lights, like a giant gray tarantula in early evening,
tense with near-misses and brilliant collisions, its movement as frantic as its mind.

The Reckoning

No one is truly dead until
they are no longer loved.
—Theophile Gautier

When your number's up,
it's up. Fortune purses
its lips and blows you out.
It's the oncoming stumble,
the Nature of things.

One minute you feel bubbles
in your brain, and then
the skull fills with
ginger ale. Pale, in pain,
you do your life's inventory.

Then only the accounting remains.
After a few years, even your
friends lose the details of your face,
eloquent distillations crumble,
and your presence fades.

There was much to answer for,
and the mistakes still grow
smaller and smaller in the distance,
as if you had abandoned them,
lumbered them on

retreating trucks, and numb,
numbered among them, your
defeated feelings that live now
in flight. Life was so simple
and fleeting, filled with clichés

and minor keys, small clues
dribbling away the magician's prestige,
and frayed, artful dodges protecting
one from the truth, that the living
are permanently enslaved

in whatever story they deign to tell,
an escalating wreck that drizzles
out into the air as the soul mists over,
wondering what next as the casualties
flame serenely on the path behind.

The Throat Singers of Tuva

Stupefied
And rolling down
The steep raves
I write
The Constitution
Of no authority
The history
Of ecstasy
Like the waves
Endlessly battered
Buttressed
From behind
By formlessness
And ahead
The only
Jagged choice
Is to carve
Themselves
Against the rock
And in doing so
Shape their
Opposite
Into the shore
And to speak
Of this woe
In thunderous
Tones

Like the blind
Throat singers
Their voicebox
Three notes
Locked between
Siberia and
The Gobi Desert
Breathing out
Rhomboids
And rain dances
Like turtledoves
In a drought
Making misty
The wobbly triangle
Of overwhelming
Fragrances
Coming from
The hidden source
No reference
To the Captain
No map
To chart
The ascent
More native
Than the Indian
More Indian
Than the sea

Running with the Bulls

in memory of Manolete

Tightly strung, like the neck of a guitar,
dancing with a ton of charred fury,
a matador does not slouch or feint,
or couch his gestures to the gallery
with satirical intent. The Beast

does not repeat its mistakes
until its enemy, a jeweled reed
in the wind, is in full focus,
popping out of the cushion of his cape
like a pin, his doomed eyes
shaded with delirium.

In love with Death, or so it seemed,
wise flies' black buzz streaming over his life
like the high tide's meticulous fuzz,
gored and awash in blood,
the storm's pageantry pushed him

out past the breaking point,
his prayers replaced by the sound of wings,
in love with the rent fabric of his own singing,
the reef snapping off the wave's soft seam,
holding his broken body aloft

as the sky filled with bloody petals,
riddling his coffin with red hail,

67

three days of dirges and his salty animal's
swollen blue smell, weightless
in the swirling mania,
running with the bulls.

Coffin Not Included

Gradually the world shuts you out,
your plum skin dapples and craters,
effectively exhausted by holding back
the waterfall that is a human being.
There is no getting used to sorrow;
every encounter, like the rungs of a ladder
lap higher and harder until the rails
turn to eels in your hands and escape
as ropes of smoke, weary of the body
and its constant demands. The walls
between this world and the next
are leaky as an old rowboat.
Heated commerce passes between them,
a musical wind, ribbons of distress
wound into our bones by ghosts.
Music can pass for conversation,
says things not entirely human,
beyond the realm of words, notes
hanging on their wires like unruffled birds.
How we are usually complicit in
the things we complain about, and yet
we have so little control over what we create.
Music makes me do just what it wants me to.
Furry arroyos, full of cactus shadows,
know that among the holies,
there is more than one ghost.

A Poem in the Shape of Tulsa

(for Ron Padgett)

Reading these remarkable
Translations of Reverdy
And stuck for
Two weeks in stinking Oklahoma
Her panhandle a paradox acrostic
Like a handshake turned into a karate chop
Oklahoma still likes Ike
Still makes rooms big enough
To house a horse
Accidents here are emulsions
Negotiating the
Stairways of desire
Second generation parachutes
Rally round the family
In the middle of the road
In the matrix of America's
Bizarre cultural breakdowns
And nothing is lost
Things are more like they are now
Than they ever were
Like poor Tulsa long dead
Choked on oil cash and gun flow
The ghosts from 1921
Sliding through the side streets
Like greased mannequins
Mocha babies in their arms
Moaning no

Old Hickory Gets the Bends

Hermitage, 1845

The riptide gripped and would not let go.
Stumpy Picard, the angel from Charleston,
swam with me. My mother was there, brother
and father as well, swallowing their bruises
with great gulps and pointing toward the shore.
Long dead, they were little help. Sometimes
what is felt is just not so. The strain I am under,
by and for the people. I am the fucking Republic,
I told Nicholas Biddle, and will kill this bank
even if it kills me. I am Jesus in the Temple,
Democracy's Damocles, and a fistful of coins
means nothing, because the mothers adore me.

Soon I will be released and summoned, this dream
I cannot waken from. Calhoun and Clay could devise
their plays, but Gentlemen, South Carolina will not
secede; if this insurrection is successful, then what is
the fate of the Union? What treasonous weasel
would incur the wrath of the Great Mother?
I have murdered a mountain of men for her,
built a Trail of Tears, mastered the buffalo and rid
the prairie of savages, speculators and parasites.
By Jefferson, this slander will not stand; just as
Florida fell to progress, so too must these Confederate
Jacobites, sand fleas that will start an itch in England

and spoil the view of the world. But why am I always
called to do the grooming? Is one blubbering man
without fear a backbone to string legislation upon?

This bottomless water I'm wandering through has
bent me and built a fortress from my breath.
At fourteen I was tossed, an orphan, upon the waves
of fortune, and a vital center of action burned in me.
I knew the majority were to govern. I was their
instrument and made it so. Self-righteousness is easy
and cheap in retrospect, but Justice does not write
History, chiefs and generals do. In this evil current
I fear the worst, without Rachel who was first and last,

and whose dignity was burst by lies and cursed journalists.
Were there not steel balls buried beside my heart and
shattered shoulder, I would stare down the barrel
of my pistol and silence this malevolent drivel.
There are no enemies in the cemetery, but how might
I manage this darkness? Though my faith in the people
has never wavered, I cannot see the land, my hands
are like doves escaped from the cage of my chest.
Blown to bits, this fuzzy air sharpens its Death on me
and I splash forward, trying to gather its razors in my arms.

God Gives Us Each a Song

The apple worm's entire world
is only the size of his apple.

Some people never venture off
the half-acre of their lawn.

When turkeys mate, they probably
think of swans, though the I

is deeply mysterious and hidden,
its "other" rarely listening; and

in the belligerent meat of our brain
there is a terrible reckless precision,

a controlled mayhem, chaos in a box;
and men spend themselves looking

for its source, listening for the pox
to creep in. But the mulish trespass

after the storm's hoopla can reveal
silver lights sewn in tiny chainmail,

trapping a headless shadow in self-portrait,
or see the tracks of white birds diminish,

swallowed by the sea's swell, their little
forks pointing north, *like that.*

And we feel outward, forgetting our
pulse, searching for anything clear

and certain, like a cat's tedious measured
pad across a skinny fallen log. *Like that*

the bifocals fog and a fingerprint lands,
then vanishes slowly. Listen to Coltrane

swinging through Cole Porter like a mad
top hat tossed haphazardly across a frozen

pond by the wind, making half-moons
in the snow as it lights, *like that.*

I hear you, she whispers, I hear you,
but I am not this abstraction, bounced

forever, as my geography leans in,
time given over to nothingness,

the time that prefigures Milky Ways
and comets scattered like rice

from the offering plates of the over
lapped universal chances, the same

ashes that dissolve in rivers that run
our bodies, that give us voice,

the worm's tiny groan as it pops out
of the apple's skin and finds itself

alone, filled with the right
of the Spirit to be known.

The Silence

Off the blue marble come mosaics of radio waves,
in hopes of communication with residents of deep space,
or travelers on expedition who might need a cool drink
and a chat at an earthly waystation. In the mirror,
we confess and are broken. Kurtz massacred his
recalcitrant subjects as Leopold II so deftly did
before him. "Innocent of what?" the judge asked
Joseph K, and the purged generals who were shot
in Moscow still shouted "Long Live Stalin!" as the metal
burned into their torsos. But there are minor proletariats,
disguised as penitent revolutionaries, who see the suicides
flailing in the Seine and serialize the complicity of
all mankind. Bingham scaled the heights of Machu Picchu
hoping it held a cradle of gold, but he bypassed Vilcabamba
and landed his dirigible on the Capitol steps, his Tiffany-
bought finery a gift of the conquered Incas. We are not alone,
and cannot back out of this now present delusion.
Satellites broken off like marble tombstones in the heavy
weather weave their languid beeps among the meteors.
What happens when cultures collide is that one becomes
the quarry, and colonial galls are harnessed in the children's
DNA. They wait then in their cellar holes for words that
the Great Divide is brooked, that no more will the cardinal
hunt for its partner alone, seeking bits of feather hung like
tatters on the hidden barbs and hooks of universal directives.
The old guitar's frets are scraped for music that might rouse
the inhabitants of a shrunken Milky Way; but can we see,
as St. Mark instructed, and not perceive? Hear, and not
understand, why the broken knuckles of the skinny bone tree
will not hold apples, why the buggies might still scare the

horses, though the radio's song is perfectly tuned to
a frequency beyond confusion? Fifty years ago, Frank Drake
began to drag a net through the eerie silence, using Marconi's
gyrations to explain the perfect circles of craters on the moon,
and the silhouettes of men who danced the hotfoot on the surface
of the sun. Who, like Lucretius, thought they spied cousins adept
at a rhumba all their own, whose critical conversations scorched
the lonely administration of a sympathetic tongue. Who looked
away for only a second, and looked back to find there were none.

"If You Are Chagall . . ."

If you are Chagall
then you believe that
fish can thresh wheat.
If you are Rodin,
the gods are your
playthings and their
hands are perfect.

The total work of art
is achieved through the
soul's inner necessity,
the way music persuades
without argument.

In this world the horses
want to stand on their
back feet and walk
like a man, towering
over the human who
has infuriated them.

All the chimneys become
holy relics and the hills
raise their skirts and
cancan, with the trees
for legs and blue feet
built from pools of water,

kicking their heels as high
as the light will allow.

From the shore the boats
are dwarfed, meager vessels
whose eager travel is
blown to molecules, notes

of the sky that prompt
the boiling ocean to pound
all attempts to tame it.
Gravity has long been
banished from this kingdom,
where the moon is the

only law and the horses
walk upright into the waves.
Their riders trail like birds
in the barking wake.
Every horse is secretly,
romantically, involved with

the sea and when they
sleep they dream of
whales flying unimpeded
through the deep music.
(Fish pity the cities).

Eros Thanatos

> *No one knows where the edge is.*
> *Those that do have gone over.*
> —Hunter S. Thompson

Forever on the verge of extinction,
at what point does Venice slip
beneath the waves? A city bathed
in twilight values, with impossible
panoramas of floating mud flats,
public gardens, and domes that
wheel past with menacing velocity.
Nothing can penetrate this romance,
or numb the flute's vivacity,
dancing from the balcony
of the *Grand Hotel des Bains.*

Casanova himself was imprisoned here
between realities, in this purgatorial
airstream gathering the best and worst
in couplings of open thirst, as stray
rhetoric scattered out in small boats
and clashed with harpoons against
the holy monsters of the deep, decrepit
cardinals and ripened priests sent down
by the Holy See to quarter this defiler,
or torture confessions from that
degenerate sexual deviant.

Casanova crabbed out of his prison
cell through the ceiling, a psychologist
of decadence, counting on the advantage

of chaos after cradling so many
powdered bosoms, whose sympathy
with the precipice produced his undoing,
plagued by the perfect release, a slave
to the melodies on the balustrade,
and beauty's eventual derision.

Numb inside its redemption and awash
in a bowl of subtle analysis, Venice
is a rose afloat in a glass of water,
its petals fiercely lit from within,
reflecting the splendor of the artist,
the will to power his body through
the black canals again and again,
whose flares of recognition
sizzle through him like cymbals,
the faint brush of electric fur
from the skin of a greater animal.

Present at the Revolution

I

Washington, freckle-faced and fierce,
brought the country like a cur to heel,
used the shoemaker's son, the gypsy
prophet, and several bastard soldiers,
and fashioned their zeal to seal the
committee's ears. You're either the hammer
or the anvil, he said, and scrambled like an
awkward aristocrat. 77 million in debt, he
erased the state's burden, utility by necessity,
and made federal assumption his steering wheel.
Paused in parade like a pop star, he walked along
the Potomac with Hamilton and Madison, held
the hands of slaves and bade them farewell, but
acquiesced to the southern Jacksons until 1808
and let the distressed race dangle, fault lines
blighting the democratic lantern that shined
on Mother Liberty. The bloody offspring
dropped stillborn on the bed, a throbbing
caul on the baby nation's head.

II

Jefferson, appalled at the guillotine's perfection,
smelled a monarch in every water closet
and saw fit to rent the tissue of machinations,
stripping the gears of government that were
finely tuned as a clock, and taking stock of
the Constitution's banking wobble, he reduced
the rabble's roar to a murmur, and used
their squabbles to levy a tax on bread and booze
and shoes that froze the farmer on his hoe
and made the mercantile almighty.
The ball of liberty bounced around the globe,
but the dragon's teeth sewn in the storm of Bastille
sprouted monsters that marched on London and built
an emperor from their spittle. Jefferson paid a poet
to slander Hamilton and retired to Monticello,
awaiting his dismemberment. Buttered by the comforts
of his farm and the bosom of maid Sally, Burr's bullet
did the deed instead, and the peacock, in full splendor,
came flying from his nest.

III

Adams, in the shadow of a legendary General,
choked on his office like a termite on a splinter,
his Federalist credentials assailed by friend
and Republican foe. The bulldog of the
Continental Congress rowed back toward Britain
as Monsieurs X, Y and Z robbed ship after ship
in the Caribbean and demanded tribute.
The Republic tilted as the citizens shouted
for Samson Adams to slay the Philistine French
with the jawbone of Jefferson, but John
stumbled across the seditious aliens and raised
an army that flailed at ghosts. He imprisoned
the muckrakers and sublimated the most extreme
members of his own Cabinet. Trapped in his trench,
the President ducked and Burr saved his powder
for another day. Adams slunk home, a shattered croc
from the Chesapeake swamp, in his head a frenzy,
his last gift to his country, another king,
his sober son Quincy.

Being, Non-Being, Becoming:
The First Hummingbird of the Summer

The dream of the man who believed
he was a butterfly that was dreaming
it was a man that dreamed of a butterfly.
The cheval mirror holds an image of a black-
shrouded senorita holding a mask that hides
her eyes. She is holding the mask by its stem,
like a rose stripped of its leaves and flower,
but blooming into a black mask with silver sequins
surrounding the eyes of a senorita. Soul signs slip
into the background.

                    Nobody is prepared to die
for a principle, though the whole world obeys
the sway of beauty. If we were able to understand
our first word, it would invariably be I, I mean myself,
not mama or papa, whose principles are rarely defined.
The saffron curtains, hanging like sheets of butter,
blow subtly in the open window, and I am outside,
in the garden, swimming in pure light, irrigating my
mind with the glint and glister of raging color,

when the first hummingbird of the summer,
whose lace wings strain and conquer the stern
principles of gravity, turns its beak from the flower
and faces me, feints a thrust and causes my stumble
backward, two hundred and forty pounds of flesh
wincing at the threat from two ounces of fury packed

behind a knitting needle, my nose no match for
the tiny blur's lightning-loaded machinery or
stealthy intention.

Even in the nose there is erectile
tissue, which may explain why the nostrils flare
even before the sex has begun, or why the right dose
of spice makes men stiffen and ladies misty, melting
all the assorted mixtures, smells, temperatures, touches
and gales of imagined perfumes into leading weak-kneed
partisans of pleasure by the proverbial nose.

When Nijinsky leapt twelve feet in the air, before a group
of astonished patrons, he said he could smell the lilies
of Heaven. When Nureyev asked his teacher if he could
be a dancer, he was told that he had the nose for it.
My own Irish proboscis has lead me into this stand
of flowering oaks, a butterfly the size of a man
trying to enter this blossoming world, dreaming of a word
that might transform his body into light, a mortal merger
with this natural portal, entry blocked by a hummingbird.

The Tipping Point

I sit stock still, watching
the curved soap sweat,
surrounded by villagers
who gather up the mountain
with their hands.
There is a hole in my ceiling
and freaks come through it.

Who creates the Gods?
Who burps the baby God,
nourishing the Deity with
dishes of scrambled stars?

The sky made of cereal
lets the moon nestle
its sliver like half a banana,
and buoyed by auroras,
it rises free of gravity into
the groggy center of our scene.

Random, prey to indulgence,
Man was inside the carbon
atom asking to be released.
Myths are public dreams.
Dreams are private myths.
The sacred places are where
eternity shines, dismembered
through the flakes of time.

We enter the deepest sleep,
the last one, wide awake.
Man did not come from the Earth
and does not command it.

He is exactly the same age
as the dirt and numbers
himself among its minions,
feral, full of sorrow, and in
perfect rapture with our eerily
singular planet, which is being
sucked ever closer to the sun.

Cinema Xanadu

Reality is privileged, and for the cinephile,
it is not enough to make love to Rita Hayworth;
it must happen in black and white.
Peeling back the layers of the dream,
how could reality possibly compare?
Seeing life inside a frame intensifies its effect.
Is Art content or form? The decisive moment
is rendered less dramatic by the character actors
scurrying away across the street to their cluttered
apartments and heating bills, like some French
New Wave film, underexposed and lit badly,
revealing the schizophrenia and compulsion.

Visionary experience is neurosis, or is it?
Does the cat lead the bell around its neck,
or is it lead? What is normal? Does the
treatment of psychosis entail the tamping down
of intense experience? What filmmaker would
be a party to that? How many homicides are
constructed by the crunching popcorn, or the
cell phone that continues to beep?
In dreams begin superstitions, and
suspended belief bolsters the frail
body against the everyday exhaustions.

These are not front row people.
The book will never be better than the movie.
The real reason that the characters die is because
God is jealous and has not managed to create perfection.

Thus the theater traps the beautiful fluttering minds
in its assorted gelatins. The nightmare will not be
recalled for its damaged aspect ratio.
The Elephant Man in the makeup chair is not interesting.
La Dolce Vita cannot happen in Japan. The Taxi Driver
in South Africa will not stalk the presidential candidate,
or forswear his allegiance to a 13-year-old prostitute.
His ticket stub will not be saved for posterity.

The pleasure dome that Kubla Khan decreed
in Xanadu was a movie palace with servants
dressed as Sophia Loren and Brigitte Bardot,
Gina Lollobrigida and Marilyn Monroe.

A Rolling Story

Late May, and this rolling story
gives us river roads
and incurable disorders, a suicide
whose bullet wound resembles
the Madonna, or a man with no legs
who designs the perfect shoe.

Place your hands over your eyes
and the mind becomes a picture house.
Place your fingers between the fingers
of another and the tangle ripens into love.
A grouse explodes from the brush
when the fingers are loosed,

its feathers make a pillow for a doll
whose child is blind. Art is incurable,
and brutish, and it decides if the river
will lay comfortably in the furrow
of its bed or take the congruent road
for its own and render it invisible instead.

The jubilee of the human form
makes light surrender to its need,
and no diploma makes its lonely valleys
settle and no master makes it breathe.
A woman with no arms learns
to paint by flexing her toes,

the way a poisoned garden will collapse
and produce a perfect rose.
If death is the mother of beauty, and stars
are born to burn out, then the river
is excused its cruelty as it
quietly swallows the town.

The Arab Spring

Jihad

The twanging ragas
of Arabia bang
aboard camels on
cliff trails balanced
daintily above exploding
sea tides and dunes
of knife-carved
apricot moonscapes
sifting inland amid
rolling bellies of
gritty Yemeni wind
a camel's futile bellow as
the sand cloud burrows in

For those who deride
the beauty in this world
they are not blind
but have stalled
cannot move through
the series of unceasing
transformations feathered
throughout their line
of sound and sight
the sawed-off incompletions
repeatedly battling
to form a strategy
to build, fan, and fuel a fire

The Arab Spring

Mourning The Morning
After Driving A Drone
Through The Heavens
On The Shore Of Oman

I

What is more lonely,
the woman in the burqa
on the beach being
chased by the skinny
javelin of her shadow,
or the trapeze bar
as it swings empty,
back and forth,
in the sea wind?
Or is it the curtain
of the waves
playing peek-a-boo
with the disappearing
shoreline, or the wind
itself, whose way is lost,
pushing here and there,
unsummoned and wandering
through the vast world,
its transparent soul unable
to hold close any fire
it happens to find?

II

I stare at the sea
like Ulysses, but I
cannot return to base.
Forms escape me
and I am lost, trembling
in the shadows
of the tribe's motion.
Today I am flitting
through old photographs
of anonymous families,
for sale at the marketplace
beneath a whale-shaped tent
that is swimming away
from the beach and
swallowing the barkers.
I gather the scattered nets
and free the dying weeds.
The blue pages of my life
fly out and are lost
in the immense azure tresses
of an endless boiling sea.

Creationism

In the Western distance,
a valley away from the Matterhorn,
where the tectonic plate of Africa
has mounted its European counterpart,
gravity is greater at this horrifying center,
and one must fight not to disappear,
to be swallowed by the earth itself,
rather than drown in the tears
of someone else's stupid truth,
pushing over the edge of your own
shifting existence. The memorials
to mortality, planted at the crossroads
and perched on bridges crossing rivers,
are the attempts, out of an acrobatic loneliness,
to gain the attention of a distant drunken deity
whose fossils assault the myth of his memory.
Out of the volcanoes belching diamonds
and continents, the Earth's fiery heart is
slowly exposed, the organ that has poisoned
its own atmosphere and crushed the bones
of one age to fuel the mutations of the next,
between floods and glaciers scratching
their backs on the mountains as they press
canyons of granite a few inches every second,
ruled by the wise blood of a ruby-hearted planet,
beating for billions of years, whose reason
is unknowable and burns because it can,
tormented as the men whose resting skeletons
it has formed and stirred the sticks of confusion
like dynamite in their flesh.

The Startling Invention of Chairs

I

The startling invention of chairs helped
the colony collapse in an orderly fashion
and Great Africa, saddled with satellite sagas
in every capital, let the day be judged by the
evening and given pause, by the crocodile's
snout on the horizon and the sun snapped
shut in its jaws; the people covered themselves
with ash left over from the sacking of the
Silk Road, flakes of pillowy gray, lightly
dusting the llama pin comprised of blood
diamonds on the dashing lady's velvet lapel.
Rappelling down Victoria Falls, Lord Stanley's
poetry gave no offense, his murders did not
condense the achievement of Zanzibar, and so
history's novice, an equal of Hillary or Columbus,
was the first continental astronaut sardonically
circling the green orb in static space, little
stellar beeps burped by the module as it
leaped over the evening star and the wages
of that destruction paid in spades for
the black instructor conducting his experiments
on Dragon Mountain and Mobile, Alabama.

II

"No one loves an armed missionary," said
Robespierre as he burned the King's dictionary,
so that the nation might thrive in spite
of character assassinations by the steamy right
wing, lacerations of truth stinging momentarily
for the politician who believes what he spins,
both chins, in complete agreement, shimmy
over his collar like a pair of dancing wallabies.
Dithering with a zither, the senator practices
his talking cure on the chimney sweeps and
the children, doing what he must for the love
of his audience and the freedom that love affords,
accords given governance over the unbroken broccoli
in their skulls. The divine participants belabor
the misprecision of the colonial system and
the people shoulder the awaiting blunders, the
trophies of forbidden wonder, the booty of Eden
squirreled away for a rainy day, mountains
of skeletons and anonymous gelatin, towers
of incumbents groping blindly in the disciplined
cherry chambers. Coattail riding, social climbing,
statesmen abhor a vacuum, their nervous tics
informed by dog whistle politics, their whinny
and wave like a cloth upon a pane, washing
the air clear of evidence, inventions, everything.

Acknowledgments

The author gratefully acknowledges the following magazines and journals where many of these poems first appeared (or are forthcoming), sometimes in slightly altered form, or as a section of a greater whole:

American Literary Review — "Rembrandt's Mirror" and "The Agnostic"

Antique Children — "Cinema Xanadu"

Asheville Citizen-Times — "Coffin Not Included"

Black Renaissance Noire — "Assuming the Conception," "The Future of An Illusion," and "Present at the Revolution"

Black Mountain Review (Ireland) — "The Arab Spring"

Broad River Review — "The Blues"

Cave Wall — "The Silver Surfer"

Cerise Press — "The Silence"

Colorado Review — "Lincoln's Life Mask" and "God Gives Us Each A Song"

Comstock Review — "On The Boardwalk" and "The Blue Teen On Train 52"

Connotation Press — "Election Day at the Grand Canyon" and "The Brides of Christ"

Cutthroat — "The Night Train To Omega"

Ecotone — "The Force Of Compassion"

Fresh Magazine — "The Reckoning"

Hampden-Sydney Review — "European Political Discourse and the Paranoid Style"

Hunger Mountain — "Being, Non-Being, Becoming" and "The Birthmark"

Indiana Review — "A Rolling Story"

International Poetry Review — "Gaudi" and "Easter In Palestine"

Iodine Poetry Journal — "The Seven Islands of Izu," "A Navel in the Middle of the World," and "Running With The Bulls"

Main Street Rag — "Rendition and The White Dwarf" and "Using The Enemy's Arrows"

North Carolina Conversations — "The Exile," "Lincoln's Life Mask"

Nantahala Review — "A Poem In The Shape Of Tulsa"

Pisgah Review — "Extraordinary Popular Delusions and The Madness of Crowds" and "The Tipping Point"

Poetry East — "Gray Power"

Portland Review — "The Startling Invention Of Chairs" and "Henry VIII"

Quarterly Literary Review (Singapore) — "Nearing Havana"

Rivendell — "Appalachia"

Shenandoah — "If you are Chagall…"

Solo Cafe — "The Director"

South Carolina Review — "Old Hickory Gets The Bends"

Southern Poetry Review — "Nanking, 1937"

Takahe (New Zealand) — "Eros Thanatos"

Victoria Press — "The Throat Singers of Tuva"

"The Blues" also appeared in the anthology, *The Poetics of American Song Lyrics* (Univ. of Mississippi Press, 2012), edited by Charlotte Pence. "If You are Chagall…" also appeared in *Far From the Centers of Ambition: The Black Mountain College Anthology* (Lorimer Press, 2012), edited by Lee Ann Brown and was featured on NC poet laureate Kathryn Stripling Byer's blog, *Here, Where I Am.* "Lincoln's Life Mask" also appeared in the *The Best Of Poetry Hickory* anthology, edited by Scott Owens. "The Agnostic" is included in *The Best of Poetry Lincolnton* anthology, due out in 2013. "The Night Train To Omega" is also published in the *Best of the Block Island Poetry Project* anthology, which will appear in 2013, edited by Lisa Starr.

About the Author

Keith Flynn (www.keithflynn.net) is the author of six books, including five collections of poetry: *The Talking Drum* (1991), *The Book of Monsters* (1994), *The Lost Sea* (2000), *The Golden Ratio* (Iris Press, 2007), and *Colony Collapse Disorder* (Wings Press, 2013). Flynn's popular collection of essays, *The Rhythm Method, Razzmatazz and Memory: How To Make Your Poetry Swing* (2007) was published by Writer's Digest Books.

From 1984 to 1999, Flynn was lyricist and lead singer for the nationally acclaimed rock band, "The Crystal Zoo," which produced three albums: *Swimming Through Lake Eerie* (1992), *Pouch* (1996), and the spoken-word and music compilation, *Nervous Splendor* (2003). He is currently touring with a supporting combo, "The Holy Men," whose album, *LIVE at Diana Wortham Theatre*, was released in 2011.

Flynn's award-winning poetry and essays have appeared in many journals and anthologies around the world, including *The American Literary Review, The Colorado Review, Poetry Wales, The Cuirt Journal* (Ireland), *Takahe* (New Zealand), *Poetry East, The Southern Poetry Review, Margie, Rattle, Shenandoah, Word and Witness: 100 Years of NC Poetry, Crazyhorse,* and many others. He has been awarded the Sandburg Prize for poetry, the ASCAP Emerging Songwriter Prize, the Paumanok Poetry Award and was twice named the Gilbert-Chappell Distinguished Poet for NC.

Flynn is founder and managing editor of *The Asheville Poetry Review,* which began publishing in 1994. For more information, please visit: www.ashevillepoetryreview.com.

Colophon

This first edition of *Colony Collapse Disorder*, by
Keith Flynn, has been printed on 70 pound
paper containing a percentage of recycled fiber.
Titles have been set in Papyrus type, the text in
Adobe Caslon type. All Wings Press books are
designed and produced by Bryce Milligan.

On-line catalogue and ordering:
www.wingspress.com

Wings Press titles are distributed
to the trade by the
Independent Publishers Group
www.ipgbook.com
and in Europe by
www.gazellebookservices.co.uk